Rescue Me Jesus

Klem Nazier

BookLeaf Publishing

India | USA | UK

Presentation by *BookLeaf Publishing*

Web: www.bookleafpub.com

E-mail: info@bookleafpub.com

ISBN: 9789357446600

First edition 2022

DEDICATION

I dedicate this book to Jesus Christ my Lord
and Saviour.

ACKNOWLEDGEMENT

I want to thank everyone who has supported my poetry writing. Thank you friends, family and church who have encouraged me to continue writing for God.

PREFACE

The reason I wrote this book is because there are people in this world that can relate to the feelings expressed. I want them to know that they are not alone in their thoughts. The aim is to press into Jesus no matter what life throws at us. God is our forever strength and joy.

Worry

I come before you and kneel on my knees.
I ask you Jesus to take my panic and worry away
with you please.

Feel me with your peace as I trust in you alone.
Thank you God for grace as I know your "still"
on the throne.

My mind needs restoring, Lord I know you can
heal.
I come to you with my anxiety that I deeply feel.

I am kneeling at your precious feet, this is where
I lay.
Please I ask Jesus to show me the right way.

Instead of worry, I ask for peace.
Instead of panic, I ask for release.

A release of darkness that clouds my soul.
A release of suffering so that you can take
control.

I don't know

Lord Jesus, I don't know what to say.
Please I beg to show me the way.

I am praying hard, I am following your word.
I intently request to show me I'm heard.

When I am lost for words, my heart skips a beat.
But I pray to you God for my sentence to be
complete.

I don't know how to talk, I don't know how to
speak.
Why do I feel like my words of prayer are so
weak?

Lord when I don't know anything, I ask for the
Fire.
And to lift my praise up higher and higher.

I love you Lord even in the doubt.
Loving you in the mystery is what your faith is
all about.

Thank you

All of your creation is truly devine.
Lord when I have nothing, I thank you for what is mine.

From sleeping in a bed, instead of the floor.
To my friends and family that I adore.

Thank you for eyes to see and ears to hear.
Thank you for your powerful presence when I have fear.

Thank you for giving us a life, thank you for your death.
Though my health is not perfect, thank you for lungs so that I may take a breath.

When we do wrong, thank you that you forgive.
Thank you for dying so that we may forever live.

Noise

There's so much noise inside my head, it's so
hard to hear.
What I learn today goes out the other ear.

I can't seem to concentrate, it's hard to think
straight.
My shoulders are heavy, they carry so much
weight.

Every thing is noisy, I just want rest.
The only thing I want to hear is the beating in
my chest.

Stillness, peace, calmness and bliss
This is what I desire, this is what I miss.

I want to focus on you Lord, please help clear
my head of distraction.
I can only do things through you God, please
help me take action.

Feel me with peace, the kind to be still.
So I can overcome any mountain and any steep
hill.

Lord I love you, please lead me with direction.
and forgive me for my wrongs and feel me with
correction.

Lonely

I prayed to God and I worshiped his name.
Yet I don't feel any better, I just remain the same

I feel so down and never in the presence of time
How can daily life feel like such a climb

I feel so lonely, I do everything on my own
I pretend that I'm okay but I'm tired of doing
everything alone

I keep having flash backs of all the good times
we shared
Wishing I could feel that again when I am paired

It hurts so much, I don't know how to explain
The never ending thoughts cause me tremendous
pain

Will I ever be happy .. can't remember the last
time I had a true smile on my face
I want someone to take up my time and to take
up my space

Not good enough

There's this feeling that I cannot shake.
I don't know how much longer I can take

I don't apply for jobs that I want because I think
I will fail.
Even if I get the job of my dreams, I would
probably bail

Because I've done it before, who says I won't do
it again
I always repeat history from way back then

I will never reach my goal, or fulfil my dream.
Of being a successful leader and running an
awesome team

I'm so weak, I don't have discipline to rule over
me
Instead I give in and let temptation take over me

Why do I think like this, what's wrong with my
mind
I beg you Lord Jesus, please help me to find

The way to live in this unholy surrounding

Cause when I get tempted my heart can't stop
pounding

But I'm saved by Christ, these thoughts are not
mine
I don't want my thinking to hinder my shine

Forgiveness

In order to receive forgiveness, you must forgive
mankind
What's done is done, you must move on, as life
cannot rewind

Forgive their sins though they have treated you
wrong, because God will do you right
But if you do not forgive and choose to hold on,
you might miss out what God has for you insight

What you have forgiven, I have forgiven, all
done insight of Christ sake
As God will know what is unfair and will give
your heart a break

Forgive your self, as you are hurting, you don't
need to bare that pain no more
God will show you the right way and will open
up your closed door

God will heal your heart and your soul, if you
choose gods path to live

He will give you peace in your soul, if you
choose to forgive

To the world life seems unfair but God will
never forget your pain
For God knows what's done in the earthly body,
so trust that he shall reign.

Negative verses Positive

According to the world, gold and power is the ultimate prize.
Along with sex, self-pleasure, alcohol drugs, the power of evil under disguise.

Only the blood of Jesus Christ will feel my empty void.
All pain and suffering I have, will be forever destroyed

When your lamp is burning, the more satan will tempt and entice.
Living and breathing God in our daily will come at a worldly troubled price.

But my lamp will burn deep and it will shine so very bright.
When all enemies look my way, they will be blinded by the light.

What about if people laugh at me and spread rumours behind my back?

The stronger our love for God, the more our
enemies will attack.

If you are conflicting between God and the
world and you're sitting on the fence.
Just remember, Psalms 18. The Lord is my rock.
He will always be at our defense.

Please God forgive me, as my body is filled with
desire to lust.
How can I be worthy of God when I feel so dirty
and disgust.

In scriptures it says, I can do all things through
Christ so I will resist the temptation to sin.
Because God has already won the battle so we
will continuously win

I'm always wishing to be a lotto winner, always
wishing for more wealth.
I will never get better. What is wrong with my
health?

Though when the body needs healing. I know, I
will be restored.
Jeremiah 30, I will restore your health and I will
heal your wounds declares the Lord

I need another hit, a pill, a lighter to burn my
smoke.
But the only thing that should be burning is the
fire of God and to be woke.

Only through you Lord, I will pass the tempted
test.
Because I trust and obey you Lord, for that I will
forever be blessed

I feel like everything in my life is going so
terribly wrong.
I only feel God's presence for the duration of one
song.

However, do not fear, ask for God's presence as
your request.
Exodus 33. My presence will go with you and I
will give you rest

I will never be successful or have a career, I'm
so stupid and so dumb.
And all this pain and suffering has made me feel
so complacent and so numb.

No. I will succeed in life because I am confident
and smart.
Psalm 37, delight yourself in the Lord and he
will give you the desires of your heart.

What about if I lost my virginity before
marriage? That makes me feel like I'm no longer
pure.
I will never find a Christian partner. I'm so ugly
and insecure.

But just watch me, I will walk down the aisle
with a dress pure as white.
Because in John it says, when we confess our
sins, they will be washed away without a sin in
clear sight

 guess what Satan? It's time for Christians to
fight back and take a stand.
 We will continue to follow God even though at
times, we may not understand.

Corinthians 6 says, I was bought with a price.
The death of the Son of God, the ultimate
sacrifice.

Isaiah 43. Fear not, for I have redeemed you, I
have called you by name, You are mine.
Thank you my personal lord and savior, my God
you are truly divine.

Feeling left out

You know what's worse then feeling alone? Is
feeling alone in a clique.
When you feel like your given a different tone,
in other words, you've received the flick.

Your not like us, you weren't here from the start,
please move on and don't look back.
The feeling of not being a part, is something in
this world we lack.

Just because we don't speak your language,
means you shouldn't try speak mine.
We are family in Christ, please act like Jesus,
because God would never decline.

We all want to feel included, we want to feel
loved. This is why it's important to combine.
So we can grow into multiplications, grow into
something that can brightly shine

Brothers and sisters in Christ means something.
Would you ever leave out yourself?
If the answer is no, then please do one thing.
Don't leave anyone else hanging on the shelf.

People are special, there is so much rival, it
would be a shame if people felt left out.
When a new person walks in, make them family.
This is what Jesus is all about.

Move forward and never look back

Lord help me to let go of all my hurts and pain.
As I know if I move forward there is so much
more to gain.

When I let go of the past, I know you will pay
me back.
As I move forward you will guide me on the
better track.

My best days are ahead, please help me to travel
light.
I want to let go of what's weighing me down so I
don't lose focus of what's in sight.

I pray that I start each morning a new and fresh
for the days ahead.
To keep the wound closed and leave behind
what's dead.

Disciple my thoughts and change the channel to
what is pure.

I know you give beauty for ashes, for that I am secure.

Let the bitterness go

Its impossible to enjoy the wonders of life and to truly live,
without Gods power and strength to quickly forgive.

Please Lord be my vindicator when I have no peace.
May all the bitterness I hold in my chest be great release.

Letting go of what's done me wrong is just the very start.
I know there's many blessings ahead if I hold a pure heart.

I don't want life to hold me back and turn me into something bitter.
Show me what's in my way so I do not become a quitter.

Thank you for all my gift of days, I ask that they are joyfully spent.
Cast out every negative feeling I hold of bitterness and resent.

Women out there

There are women out there that are not okay!
Fighting so HARD to see the light of day.

Heavily trying to keep their head held high.
But every smile exposed it just a little white lie.

There are women out there that feel pain from childhood.
SCREAMING to be heard but sadly misunderstood.

They hide behind their experiences and use it as an EXCUSE.
And feel pain 10 times WORSE because they have suffered from all types of abuse.

There are women out there who have lived through sexual assault.
And feel like their relationship is a never-ending CULT.

There are women out there that find it hard to reach to the top because they don't have a DICK.

Or because they're not wearing any makeup,
they look physically sick.

There are women out there that cry themselves
to sleep every single night.
And have lost all hope in this world without a
clear vision in sight.

There are women out there that cancel plans
because they look in the mirror and convince
themselves they look like shit.
And the only way to enjoy their life is if they go
to the gym and look really fit.

There are women out there that feel incredibly
lonely in a large crowed.
Or when they're in a quiet lonely space, their
mind is PAINFULLY loud.

There are women's bodies out there that are
CONSTANTLY leaking.
From Crying to Period to Miscarriage to Sex to
RAPE.
It's just that SIMPLE…. There's no BLOODY
escape.

There are women out there that settle for less.
And think they won't get any better so they just
say YES.

There are women out there that have been
continuously stalked.
And look back every 5 minutes with every path
they have walked.

There are women out there that live in constant
fear and worry.
They don't know how to feel, so they just feel
sorry.

Don't tell us it's just that time of month or we
over think all the time.
Because thinking about our future and analyzing
our choices is not a crime.

We need EVERY SINGLE PERSON OUT
THERE to lend a helping hand.
So together we can make women feel safe and
brave enough to take a stand.

Waking up with a toxic mind

I wake up with a toxic mind, desperately waiting to change that around.
I play the Christian music straight away and listen activity to the peaceful sound.

I instantly feel better because my heart can relate.
To the lyrics they are singing in my current mental state.

I'm trying to be grateful , I'm trying to have a positive mind.
I'm telling harsh things to myself when I know I should be kind.

No matter what choices I make, I cant seem to find peace.
Lord that's the negative thinking I pray desperately to release.

Lord Jesus I cry out for a healthy mind, a healthy heart and a healthy soul.

I know I cant do this on my own so I ask that
you please take control.

24

What am I doing with my life?

I'm sitting on the ground thinking what should I
do?
Is this what life is all about, is this what my life
has come too?

Don't know what to do in the present, don't
know what to do tomorrow.
I feel like I'm just drowning in all my pity and
sorrow.

I'm nearly 25, I'm suppose to be mentally stable.
But my mind is shooting darts of thoughts
telling me I'm unable

Lord, help me to stop feeling negative and so
low.
I pray to believe in stronger hope in order for me
to grow.

Grow into something big, grow into something
strong.

Grow into a place of righteousness, a place where I belong.

26

I don't know what the future holds

I don't know what the future holds but I know I trust in the Most High.
I trust in him with all my strength, I trust in him until I die.

I don't know what the future holds, but I know it's in God's hands.
I leave it up to God Almighty, I know he has great plans.

I don't know what the future holds but I trust in what He has done.
I trust him with my heart The All Sufficient One.

Lord, I don't know what the future holds but I pray that I stop stressing.
Because I know that as long as I'm with you there will come great blessing.

Wind and Sun

Thank you for this glorious day.
Thank you for the freedom to pray.

I just want to feel at ease.
I want to feel normal, I beg you please.

My breath feels heavy, my breath feels deep.
My worry keeps me from taking a leap.

I stand in the sun and feel the wind breeze,
in the middle of the day during a lock down
freeze.

I am not sure of anything at this stage, but one
thing I know.
That I love standing in the sun and feeling this
mighty wind blow.

Feelin lost as I sit by the fence.
My minds out of control and nothing makes
sense.

Now I am lying on the grass enjoying the sun
shine on my face.

Knowing in the mess, God wants me in this
place.

I close my eyes and enjoy the peace and grace.
Remembering God gave me this time to enjoy
and to purely embrace.

Your timing is perfect, I ask that I must,
have patience in your actions, its you within I
trust.

Body as a temple

Heavenly Father, I surrender my body to you.
When I am feeling tired and old, please help me
feel brand new.

My body is yours, please make it your own.
It's yours from top to bottom and to the very last
bone.

Any ungodly thing you find, cast them out with
your power.
Treat my body with love and gentleness just like
a flower.

Take control of my body, please Lord take the
lead.
I want you in charge, this is what I plead.

My body is your home, I want the whole world
to know.
Make my body your temple, make it forever
glow.

Show me my worth

Dear God, reveal to me my full potential.
Make me feel like I am well essential.

Upgrade my confidence and fill me with a
vision.
Please help me God to always make the right
decision.

I never want to feel that I need to protect the
past.
I know you will provide me with blessings that
will forever last.

I ask that you remind me of my identity.
I thank you Lord for the gift of eternity.

I pray for boldness and Jesus to be my strength
guide.
I request that you always protect me and be by
my side.